Living Traditions
of
RUSSIAN FAITH

BOOKS & MANUSCRIPTS OF THE OLD BELIEVERS

an exhibition at the Library of Congress
May 31 – June 29, 1990

Abby Smith & Vladimir Budaragin

Library of Congress
Washington
1990

Publication of this catalog was made possible by a grant from Dr. Armand Hammer.

Smith, Abby.
    Living traditions of Russian faith; books & manuscripts of the
Old Believers; an exhibition at the Library of Congress, May
31-June 29, 1990/Abby Smith & Vladimir Budaragin.
      p. cm.
  ISBN 0-8444-0710-0
—— —— Z663.113 .S59 1990
    1. Old Believers—Soviet Union—History—Exhibitions. 2. Old
Believers—Soviet Union—Manuscripts—Exhibitions. 3. Old
Believers—Soviet Union—Liturgy—Texts—Manuscripts—Exhibitions.
4. Manuscripts, Church Slavic—Exhibitions. 5. Manuscripts, Russian
(Old)—Exhibitions. I. Budaragin, Vladimir. II. Library of
Congress. III. Title.
BX601.S59 1990
291.9'47'074753—dc20   90-20114
                                           CIP

Contents

Foreword

We at the Library of Congress were pleased to host this historic exhibition of Old Believer manuscripts. The Library of Congress, as the national library of America, collects not only the recorded knowledge of its own people, but also the historical record of all nations. America is a culture forged from many different people. America's library preserves the historic past of others so that we may understand better both our own world and ourselves.

I have taken a special personal pride in this exhibition. I have long been a student of Russian culture, interested in the religious traditions of the Orthodox Church and in the formative years of the Old Believer movement in the seventeenth century. I first saw Old Believer manuscripts in Leningrad nearly thirty years ago, and this exhibit is in many ways the fulfillment of a dream: to share some of these moving human documents with my countrymen.

It was appropriate to bring these marvelous, hand-crafted books from remote corners of the USSR to the Jefferson Building, which is in truth a living museum of the book culture of the world. We were fortunate to have items that have never before been on display outside the Soviet Union and some that have not yet been exhibited there. Books are a uniquely personal and intimate medium, through which we come into contact with the individuals who have created and used them. These volumes record the faith and illustrate the craftmanship of men and women whose tradition forms an important and neglected part of the heritage of the Russian people.

This show was conceived, curated, and mounted in less than two months. It is a sign of the improvement in relations between our two countries that such a ground-breaking exhibit could be organized so rapidly and effectively—in time for the Washington summit with Raisa Gorbacheva at the opening.

I would like to thank Dr. Armand Hammer for supporting this exhibition and publication, thus opening up yet another horizon in the field of Soviet-American cultural exchange that he has long championed in so many ways. We are also grateful to the Ministry of Culture of the USSR, which facilitated the loan and travel of these rare items; to Academician Dmitry Likhachev, whose love of Old Russian literature and of book culture inspired this show; and especially to Vladimir Budaragin of the

Academy of Sciences' Institute of Russian Literature in Leningrad and Romil Khrustalev of the Rogozh Old Believer Community in Moscow, who so generously entrusted to us the books, manuscripts, and maps that are under their care.

JAMES H. BILLINGTON
Librarian of Congress

Foreword

I am very pleased by this opportunity to address both connoisseurs and lovers of Old Russian culture on the occasion of the exhibition at the Library of Congress entitled "Living Traditions of Russian Faith: Books and Manuscripts of the Old Believers."

It seems to me that the realization of this fine collaboration bears witness to the growing interest of Americans in the culture of the Russian people. It is profoundly significant that the exhibition was opened during the visit to America of President Mikhail Gorbachev in May–June 1990—a pivotal event in the history of Soviet-American relations.

This exhibition has been exceptional in many ways. It marks the first time so many extraordinary and indeed unique items of the Old Believers have gone on display in one exhibition. It is also the first time an exhibition of such rarities has gone abroad. Never before has such an important show been organized and mounted in such a short time. All this testifies to the fact that with good will and the sincere desire to develop the spirit of cooperation, it is possible to overcome any number of complications and obstacles.

I hope this exhibit will help many Americans to understand better the roots of Russian culture, to become aware of its distinctive nature, and to look with a fresh eye at the priceless spiritual heritage of our people, a heritage which we will always strive to preserve and protect.

I am certain that this exhibit will prove to be only the first step on the road to further collaborative efforts between the Library of Congress and Soviet cultural institutions.

Let me take this opportunity to thank the Librarian of Congress, Dr. James Billington, and all of our colleagues at the Library for their brilliant work in preparing and carrying out this exhibition.

From the bottom of my heart, I sincerely wish the American people peace, happiness, and prosperity.

NIKOLAI N. GUBENKO
Minister of Culture of the USSR

SOURCES OF
OLD BELIEVER MANUSCRIPTS

In 1949, the USSR Institute of Russian Literature of the Academy of Sciences established a special archive, called the "Ancient Repository," for their collection of Old Russian literature. It has been very active in acquiring manuscripts, and in the last forty years the Institute of Russian Literature has organized over one hundred expeditions to search for books in the villages and remote communities where Old Believers or their descendants live. Most of the expeditions have been in the northern parts of European Russia, but occasionally other areas yield valuable finds as well. The stars on this map indicate the places where the books in this exhibition have been found. By far the majority of the materials gathered on expeditions are given to the institute as outright gifts. Just last year the Ancient Repository acquired 105 manuscripts that date from the fifteenth to the twentieth centuries. The manuscripts and printed books exhibited from the Rogozh Old Believer Community in Moscow are generally gifts from parishioners and represent a selection of books that are used to this day for services. This show, with additional printed and manuscript books from the rich Slavic collections of the Library of Congress, represents a unique curatorial collaboration between scholars from both the Institute of Russian Literature and the Library of Congress.

*Indicates a place where books seen in this exhibit were found.

GOSPELS *[Evangelie-tetr],* 1490s

Although there is no indication where the manuscript *Evangelie-tetr* was written, its style and design point to traditions of Novgorod icon painting and book illumination. The illumination of St. John the Evangelist shown here is similar to that found in a manuscript of 1494 that was copied at the Valaam Monastery near Novgorod. All four of the Evangelists are illuminated in this book, but the portrayal of John is distinctive in its dynamism and drastic foreshortening. These unusual effects heighten the impression of spiritual tension and inspiration, rather than emphasizing contemplation, the attitude that commonly characterized the Evangelists in Orthodox iconography. Here one can almost see John being acted upon by divine inspiration, while he in turn transmits this inspiration directly to his amanuensis, Prochoros. The scene is taken from the apocryphal book *The Journey of John the Evangelist.*

Until the middle of the 1970s, this manuscript was in the possession of the Pershins, an Old Believer family from the Vladimir region.

PERSHIN COLLECTION, NO. 1
Institute of Russian Literature, Academy of Sciences, Leningrad

BOOK CULTURE IN MEDIEVAL RUSSIA

Books first came to Russia—or, more precisely, to Rus', the homeland of the three East Slavic nations of Russia, Belorussia, and the Ukraine—in 988 when Prince Vladimir of Kiev was baptized in the Orthodox Church. The peoples of Rus' inherited from Byzantium a rich literary tradition that included a large variety of liturgical genres, as well as legal codes, musical texts, and highly developed canons of iconography and book illumination. These models were closely followed for several generations, but the East Slavs began to adapt certain basic texts and genres to their own needs and tastes. By the fourteenth and fifteenth centuries, Kiev was in decline and Moscow was emerging as a center of secular power in central Russia. Monasteries became very active in the development and spread of the cult of the book among the Russians. Often founded deep in the woods and on the remote border regions of Muscovy, these monastic outposts of pioneering clerics and lay settlers developed into the seedbed of a flourishing book culture, where individually created, highly decorated texts were produced and disseminated.

Although most religious books produced in Russia in the medieval period were written in genres that derived from Byzantine prototypes, they varied a great deal in format and design, ranging from exquisitely ornamented and bound books for use on solemn holy days to small volumes to be used for private devotion, often resembling "pocket editions." Among the most popular genres were tales of saints' lives, collections of psalms, liturgical calendars, and apostolic writings. Whether large or small, for liturgical or private use, these books displayed a passion for ornamentation that is characteristically Russian.

The introduction of printing at the end of the sixteenth century did not have much immediate impact on book production in Russia. The first book was printed in Moscow, by Ivan Fedorov, at the Printing Court in the Kremlin. Though built under the protection of Ivan the Terrible in 1553, the press was burned by an angry mob who saw in the wonder of movable type a terrifying product of evil spirits. Fedorov was forced to flee abroad, where he reestablished his press first in L'vov, and then in Ostrog. Here in 1580 he produced the first complete East Slavic Bible.

Long after the introduction of printing, Russians continued to produce hand-written books, and these manuscripts became an important vehicle for the preservation and development of folk art, especially the arts of ornamentation, illumination, and miniature painting. This manuscript tradition was especially lively among the Old Believers, a branch of Orthodoxy that split off from the Russian Orthodox Church in the middle of the seventeenth century, when the Old Believers refused to accept certain liturgical reforms and would not bow to the authority of the tsar to enforce religious conformity. The Old Believers had a special respect for books, which they revered in the same spirit as they did icons, and because as schismatics they were denied access to printing presses "to spread the Word," they developed a manuscript tradition that was vigorous and creative. Their heavily ornamented books incorporated and preserved many elements of folk art that were lost in the rest of the empire when printing became widespread. The Old Believers were great collectors of icons as well as books, and it was in fact to those native traditions, fostered by the Old Believers, that such artists as Kandinsky, Goncharova, Malevich, and Chagall turned for inspiration at the beginning of the twentieth century. This manuscript tradition plays an important, if still little studied, role in the creation of nonobjective painting and the evolution of such pivotal artistic movements of early Modernism as Constructivism and Suprematism. The books that the Old Believers produced and preserved have also been an important source for modern scholars studying the culture of Russia before the reforms of Peter the Great. Musicology, iconography, linguistics, literature, anthropology—all these disciplines have found this manuscript tradition to be a rich treasury of primary materials, and such institutions as the Academy of Sciences have been active in gathering, restoring, and analyzing the books.

ACTS AND EPISTLES *[Apostol],* late fifteenth or early sixteenth century

An *Apostol* comprises the Acts of the Apostles and the Epistles. Here, sixteen color illuminations of the Apostles Paul, James, Peter, John, Judas, Timothy, and others are included in the margins of the leaves. The beginning of each epistle is accompanied by a depiction of its writer. This iconographic style of representation—not on individual leaves or in headpieces but in the margins of the manuscript leaves—dates back to late Byzantine models. This illumination, again of St. John the Evangelist and St. Prochoros, conveys a sense of inner tranquility through their static pose and the firmness of their gaze as they look intently before them. The linguistic peculiarities of the text, the colored gamma letter, and the expressiveness of the painted figures all suggest that this volume came from the city of Pskov.

The manuscript was acquired from M. A. Epifanov, an Old Believer elder of Pskov, in 1975.

NOVGOROD–PSKOV COLLECTION, NO. 21

Institute of Russian Literature, Academy of Sciences, Leningrad

ACTS AND EPISTLES *[Apostol]*, Moscow, 1564

The *Apostol* printed in Moscow in 1564 marks the beginning of Russian printing. Although seven other printed books are known from this decade, or perhaps even earlier, none of them can be dated with certainty. Nor do we know the name of the printer for any of them. The *Apostol* is the first volume with indications of the printers' names—Ivan Fedorov and Petr Timofeevich Mstislavets—the place of publication—Moscow—and the date—1564.

Printing was slow to replace hand copying in Russia, and among Old Believers of the North printing was not common for another three hundred years. This was largely because, as schismatics, they were expressly forbidden by law to own presses or to print their literature. Old Believers who settled in the western parts of the empire, however, had access to presses across the border, and many of their liturgical books were printed.

The opening page of the Acts of the Apostles, shown here, contains a hand-colored woodcut, a form of ornamentation that became common in printed works. The severe foreshortening is meant to indicate three-dimensional space, an illusion which Orthodox iconographers would never have tried to create. The baroque floral and architectural details also betray the Western origins of this image of St. Luke.

RARE BOOK AND SPECIAL COLLECTIONS DIVISION
Library of Congress, Washington, D.C.

GOSPELS *[Evangelie-aprakos],* last third of the sixteenth century

The Gospel readings in this text—an *aprakos* Gospel—are arranged in the order they are read during each service following the liturgical calendar, and they are numbered by week and day rather than by chapter and verse, as in standard texts. Thus the first reading is from the Gospel of St. John (the last book in the standard arrangement of the four Gospels). Likewise, the sequential order of illuminations of the Evangelists differs from the standard order. The depiction of St. Mark seen here is an outstanding example of the art of the period. The gold background indicates divine illumination, and the Evangelist is thus "framed" by the light of God. The interior furniture is used not realistically, to create naturalistic space, but iconographically, to indicate that St. Mark exists in a world of harmony and contemplation, removed from the mundane cares of daily life.

The manuscript came to the Institute of Russian Literature from the heirs of Dr. V. V. Velichko, a Moscow collector.

VELICHKO COLLECTION, NO. 24
Institute of Russian Literature, Academy of Sciences, Leningrad

THE LIFE OF PETER AND FEVRONIA *[Zhitie Petra i Fevronii],* early seventeenth century

The tale of Peter and Fevronia was originally written in the 1540s by the author and hagiographer Ermolai Erasmus. It does not fit into traditional Russian saints' lives literature, however. It deals not with spiritual trials but with the love of a peasant girl from Riazan' for a prince of Murom. Various folkloric themes borrowed from Murom oral tradition are used in the story of the two lovers, and it is consequently one of the most lyrical and poetic works of Old Russian literature. More than one hundred manuscript copies of the tale still exist, dating from the sixteenth through the twentieth centuries, but illuminated manuscripts are rare. The illuminations here are done in the tradition of icon painting, with the saints in monastic garb, their hands lifted in prayer. Above is Christ Pantocrator, one hand extended in a gesture of blessing, the other holding a book.

IMLI COLLECTION, NO. 9
Institute of Russian Literature, Academy of Sciences, Leningrad

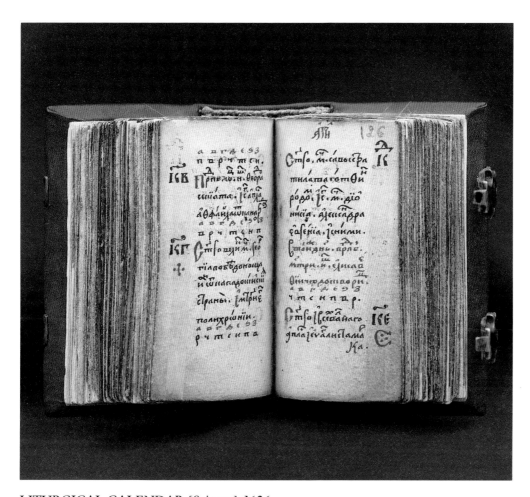

LITURGICAL CALENDAR *[Sviattsy]*, 1636

For all intents and purposes a pocket calendar, this manuscript corresponds in format precisely to its maker's intention—to encourage the owner always to have it at hand. A church calendar serves to remind mortals of their interconnectedness with the rest of the created world by enabling its readers to reflect on the liturgy of the day. This particular calendar was designed in this handy size for the times when its owner would be on pilgrimages or other journeys. As usual, the book is decorated inside with ornate headpieces and initials, but their diminutive scale lends them a special charm.

This manuscript was discovered in 1970 in the North Dvina River region, and the current binding was done during restoration in 1975. The embossing on the exterior was modeled after a piece of the original binding.

SEVERODVINA COLLECTION, NO. 57

Institute of Russian Literature, Academy of Sciences, Leningrad

ALTAR GOSPELS *[Evangelie-tetr],* L'vov, 1683 or 1690

As a rule, Old Believers did not recognize liturgical texts printed in Kiev, L'vov, or Mogilev in the western parts of Rus', because these books were sources for Nikon's church reforms and the text corrections he undertook in the middle of the seventeenth century. This introduction of "new" ritual practices was based on the liturgy of the contemporary Greek Church. At that time the Greeks were subjects of the Ottoman Turks and they themselves recognized Muscovite Russia as the last bulwark of true Orthodoxy, despite the acknowledged differences in liturgy as observed in Russia. Nikon, however, wanted to bring native practices into line with the Greek, and he declared Muscovite religious texts "tainted," owing to the many clerical errors that had crept in over centuries of copying books by hand. Supporters of the Old Faith argued, conversely, that it was the Greek Church that had strayed from its true and pious rites. In the end Nikon prevailed, and from that time only the "corrected" texts were to be printed. This copy of the Gospels is a rare exception, in that it dates from after the reforms, is printed in L'vov, and has a Western style of depicting the Evangelist sitting in a naturalistically rendered room, complete with tiled flooring, draperies, and an open window in the background. Yet it is itself an "uncorrected" text, and it is recognized by the Old Believers as canonical to this day.

OP. 475
Church of the Intercession, Moscow

DIVERGING CULTURES:
THE OLD BELIEVERS

Under Tsar Mikhail Fedorovich Romanov (1613–1645), and especially under his son Tsar Aleksei (1645–1676), Russia took an increasingly active role in European affairs. Along with military reforms designed to strengthen the country's defenses against the West, Tsar Aleksei also undertook a codification of laws, and supported his ambitious mentor and friend, Patriarch Nikon, in his efforts to centralize power within the Russian Orthodox Church. With the help of Greek and South Slavic clergy who came to Moscow in ever-increasing numbers (usually through Kiev and other centers of Orthodoxy in the Ukraine and Belorussia), the patriarch introduced reforms in the liturgy which were designed to bring Russian practice in line with what he conceived to be the more authentically patristic practice of the Greek Church. All this took place during a time of a widespread religious revival in Muscovy, led by a group of clergy called the Zealots of Piety. This movement, like the liturgical reform initiated by the patriarch, was aimed at the reinvigoration of the church and the spiritual renewal of believers. Although the patriarchal reforms were accepted by various church councils of the 1650s and 1660s, a significant proportion of the population, both lay and clerical, viewed them as unsanctified innovations and as an implicit condemnation of the piety of their forefathers. Enspirited by the religious activism of the time and encouraged by certain Zealots of Piety, many people rejected the reforms and denied to both patriarch and tsar the authority to introduce them.

The tsar, however, was prepared to back the decision of his patriarch with the force of the state: the rejection of the reforms became a political as well as a theological matter. By the 1680s, the breakaway religious movement had grown quickly, along with resistance to the government, and in 1684 Tsar Aleksei's daughter, Sophia, acting as regent for her brother Peter, promulgated laws that made adherence to the Old Belief a state crime. This decade saw the first martyrs of the schism, among them the fathers of the Old Belief — Avvakum, Epifanii, Feodor, and Lazar' — as well as members of the nobility such as Boyarina Morozova and Princess Urusova. The movement grew rapidly among the peasantry as well, as many peasants believed that the patriarch's condemnation of their generations-old practices of worship could only signify the impending end of the world.

With the emergence of a secular absolutist state under Peter the Great, and the often brutal enforcement of cultural and political reforms based on Western European models, the paths of Russian culture bifurcated. For the next two centuries, the Old Belief became a protector of cultural as well as religious dissent, also nurturing native artistic traditions and practices. When later laws allowed the Old Believers to practice openly if they registered, untold numbers refused. Registration meant paying a punitive double capitation tax, in addition to the tax on men who wore beards. Furthermore, Old Believers were forbidden to hold public office, they were not allowed to propagate their faith, and parents were not allowed to educate their own children in their faith. For the next two centuries, the Old Belief stood committed to defending the religious and cultural norms of the Tsardom of Muscovy, and Old Believers created for themselves in their isolated communities zones of freedom in which they could protect the traditions of their ancestors. The books that they copied lovingly generation after generation became one of the most important vehicles for preserving the culture they valued so highly.

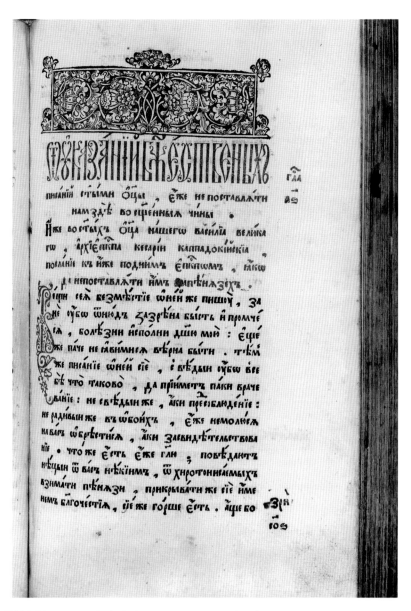

NOMOCANON *[Kormchaia kniga],* Moscow, 1650-53

The second law book printed in Russia, the *Nomocanon,* called the Pilot or Navigating Book in Russian, is a compendium of ecclesiastical and civil (i.e., Roman) laws with commentaries. It was a standard text, inherited from the Byzantine Church when Russia accepted the Greek rite in 988. Several different versions circulated in manuscript copies for centuries, until it was printed in the 1650s as part of the effort by Tsar Aleksei Mikhailovich and his government to normalize legal codes. After the Church Synod of 1651, which adopted certain reforms, this text was suppressed, and a new "corrected" edition was printed in 1653. The copy shown here contains leaves of the early version bound together with the "corrected" sections.

LAW LIBRARY RARE BOOK ROOM
Library of Congress, Washington, D.C.

AUTOBIOGRAPHY OF MONK EPIFANII *[Zhizneopisanie inoka Epifaniia]* (second part), autograph, 1670s

This small manuscript book is the work of the monk Epifanii, one of the four principal leaders of the first generation of Old Believers. He, like his three coreligionists, was burned alive in 1682 for "high crimes against the Tsar." Epifanii became the spiritual father of Archpriest Avvakum during the latter's period of exile in Pustozersk, and he blessed his spiritual son's literary efforts, including Avvakum's now famous autobiography. Avvakum, for his part, encouraged his confessor to try his own hand at writing the tale of his life and sufferings for the faith. This manuscript is the result. This copy of the autobiography, written in Epifanii's own hand, represents the second part of his life story and is one of three copies known—which is unusual, as autographs are very rare in Old Russian literature. The book was written while the monk was in an underground prison. It is not known whether this copy reached its intended addressees (the brothers Mikhail and Ieremii), or where it was kept for three centuries.

In 1971, manuscript experts found the book in the Amosov house in the village of Borok, in the Northern Dvina region of Russia.

AMOSOV–BOGDANOVA COLLECTION, NO. 469
Institute of Russian Literature, Academy of Sciences, Leningrad

GOSPELS OF TSAREVNA SOPHIA ALEKSEEVNA, Moscow, 1680s

The Tsarevna Sophia, daughter of Tsar Aleksei and the older sister of Peter the Great, ruled the Russian state in all but name from 1682 until 1689. She had an exceptional education for her time, having learned Greek and Latin, and was a great patron of the arts.

This manuscript was undoubtedly illuminated by the finest masters at the Kremlin Armory, and baroque ornamental elements, as well as the almost excessive exquisiteness of detail, show just how strong Western baroque influences were at this time. The text of these Gospels, according to legend, was written in Sophia's own hand; a short note at the end of the volume, in another hand, indirectly attests to the belief: "Sophia the Tsarevna labored over this."

The manuscript was probably given by the tsarevna to her favorite minister, Prince V. V. Golitsyn, who was later exiled by Peter to Kargopol'. A note on one of the leaves attributes ownership in the nineteenth century to the Kargopol' Transfiguration Monastery. In the twentieth century it came to the Institute of Russian Literature from Petrozavodsk.

KARELIAN COLLECTION, NO. 241
Institute of Russian Literature, Academy of Sciences, Leningrad

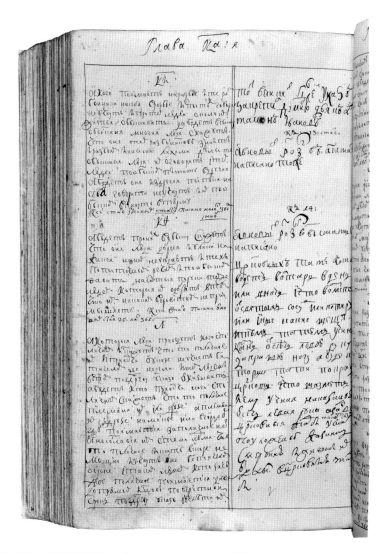

THE LAW CODE OF 1649 *[Ulozhenie]*, Moscow, 1720s

This important compilation of Muscovite secular law, completed in 1649, was originally written on an exceptionally long manuscript scroll. In this particular form of record-keeping, leaves were affixed to one another vertically and then rolled up into a scroll, a standard Muscovite practice that was changed only under Peter the Great. The law code was also published in book form when it was completed in 1649. The press run turned out to be far too small, though, and by the eighteenth century a new edition, one which incorporated the many new laws that had been promulgated under Peter, was ordered. Illustrated here is a book issued in the 1720s not by a printer but by scribes. This manuscript edition combines the codex and scroll formats in a curious way that makes it rather hard to read. In the left-hand column is the law as it appeared in 1649; to the right, usually in a different hand, are various emendations, corrections, and new decrees.

LAW LIBRARY RARE BOOK ROOM
Library of Congress, Washington, D.C.

TALE OF THE SOLOVKI FATHERS AND MARTYRS *[Povest' ob ottsakh i stradal'tsakh solovetskikh]*, last quarter of the nineteenth century

The *Tale* is derived from historical events—the seige in 1668–76 by the tsar's troops of the Solovki Monastery, the most important northern monastery and a bastion of Orthodoxy. The clergy at Solovki did not accept the reforms of Patriarch Nikon, would not submit to the authority of the state, and refused even to mention the tsar in their prayers. The monastery finally fell to the army when one monk betrayed the others, and reprisals were severe: almost all remaining men were killed, drowned, or left to die in the arctic cold. The *Tale* was written in the 1720s by Semen Denisov (1682–1740), one of the founders of the Vyg-Leksa Monastery. He used oral and written sources almost contemporary with the events themselves. The *Tale* was acclaimed in Old Believer circles and was frequently copied. Among the most prominent copiers of manuscripts in the nineteenth century were members of the Kalikin family from Vologda Province. One of the men, Fedor Antonovich, became a well-known restorer and expert on old icons and manuscripts. This manuscript is an example of his work, done in the late nineteenth century "in the olden style," with an authentic-looking pencil note about the purchase of the manuscript in Archangel in 1750, added to make the copy appear antique.

VELICHKO COLLECTION, NO. 35
Institute of Russian Literature, Academy of Sciences, Leningrad

WORKS OF ARCHPRIEST AVVAKUM, late nineteenth or early twentieth century

Avvakum (1620–1682), a zealous foe of the church reforms introduced by his one-time friend, Patriarch Nikon, was exiled first to Siberia, then to the far North. There he suffered great physical and spiritual torture until his execution by fire in 1682, which is depicted here. While in exile in Pustozersk, he wrote his autobiography, a work unique in world literature. Although he models it on the traditional genre of the saint's life, Avvakum uses a compelling and at times startling mixture of high liturgical style and biting colloquial expression. One of the key texts in the Old Believer canon, the work was hand-copied for nearly two hundred years and was published as a printed work in 1862. The boldness and expressiveness of the language struck many who read it, and Turgenev recommended it to all Russian writers as a model.

The artist of the nine miniatures in this book is the Yaroslavl' icon painter Alexander Velikanov, noted for his mastery of an ornamental style reminiscent of Palekh paintings. His work reflects the influence of the highly decorative "pseudo-Russian" style so popular at the end of the nineteenth century, and it is closer to the tradition of book illustration, with its variegated color scheme and crowded picture plane, than to the more solemn and harmonious icon-style illumination.

INDIVIDUAL ACQUISITIONS, OP. 24, NO. 16
Institute of Russian Literature, Academy of Sciences, Leningrad

A PEOPLE OF THE BOOK:
THE PRIESTLESS SECT

In Russia, as in Europe, the end of the seventeenth century was a time of great social and political upheaval that engendered in many people an anxiety that the world was coming to an end. This millenarian fever swept through Russia in the 1660s and 1670s, at the height of the schism, and some who rejected the church reforms came to believe that the reign of the Antichrist, predicted to commence in 1666 (the very year of the church council which adopted the reforms), had begun. People began to flee to the far north of the country out of fear for the safety of their immortal souls. When the tsar's army routed the monastic fortress of Solovki on the White Sea, whose inhabitants had staunchly defended the old rite, the dissenters spread even further across the remote regions of the North.

When the apocalyptic expectations of the first generation of dissenters proved to be wrong, the Old Believers were forced to come to terms with the church and the state. By the time of Peter the Great's death in 1725, they had split into two main groups, according to their understanding of the Antichrist. One group believed that the reign of the Antichrist was essentially spiritual and had already begun. This group concluded, therefore, that the Church could not exist on this earth, that the apostolic succession of the consecrated priesthood had been broken, and that men could enjoy only the sacraments of baptism and penance, since these could be administered by laymen. This branch of Old Believers, who came to be known as "the priestless," fled the tsar's kingdom and went North, where they felt they would be far from the dangerous touch of the Antichrist. There, on the shores of the Baltic and White Seas and deep in the forests, they established their communities, set up on the model of monasteries rather than parishes, as they no longer recognized the office of the priesthood.

These Old Believers in the North came to be called the Pomorians, or people from the Pomor'e (an area that embraces the shores of the White Sea, Lake Onega, and the rivers Onega and North Dvina), and the primary cultural, ideological, and artistic center of the Pomorians was the Vyg-Leksa Monastery in northern Karelia. Here a number of polemical works were created, such as the *Responses from the Pomor'e, The Vineyard of Russia,* and *The Tale of the Solovki Fathers and Martyrs.* In the eighteenth century, these communities had an influence far exceeding their size or political status. At a time when the state was aggressively inculcating Western European values and ideas in the gentry through its educational system, the Old Believers alone were looking after the educational and spiritual needs of the merchant and peasant classes. The Old Believers were busy propagating their faith in the old rite and traditional piety and spreading literacy among these two groups through what today would be called *samizdat,* or self-published literature. Moreover, the priestless Old Believers preached that the messianic and apostolic role that had formerly been played by the tsar and his church was now invested in the Russian people. This proved to be a potent idea with great influence among segments of the Western-educated elite in the following century.

The other group of Old Believers, who continued to practice their faith as they had done before the schism, were known as "the priested." They believed the reign of the Antichrist to be real, to be physical. Finding no evidence that it had yet begun, they clung to more traditional forms of worship. In most ways, their forms of worship and way of life remained just as they had been before the schism. They were not as radical in their rejection of the Russian church and empire, and they tended to settle in southern border areas and in cities, where they became important members of Russia's small industrial and merchant class.

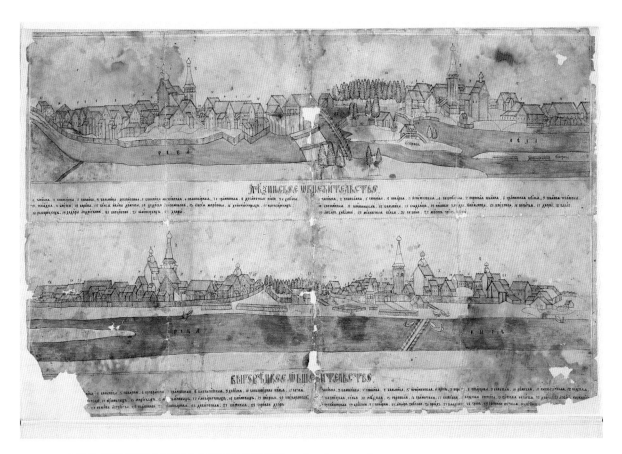

MAP OF VYG-LEKSA MONASTERY, early nineteenth century

Founded after the fall of the Solovki Monastery, the Old Believer Vyg-Leksa Monastery was established in the depths of the forests near Lake Onega around 1695 and existed until 1855. Its founder, Andrei Denisov, called it "an outgrowth of the Solovki cloister, rooted in the rule and benediction of the Solovki fathers." Vyg-Leksa became an important ideological center of the Old Belief: writers, orators, and artists flourished there and workshops for metal icon-casting and book-copying sprang up as well. A new and distinctive style of writing and book decoration, termed "Pomorian," rapidly developed. The monastery also played a significant role in the industrial development of the region.

Denisov first established the Danilov Monastery, on the Vyg River; then in 1706, a women's community was formed on a tributary of the Vyg called the Leksa. This map shows a rare panoramic view of both parts of the community at its peak, with numbered references to all the buildings and geographical features. In both the men's and the women's settlements, the scriptoria are among the largest of the buildings, testifying to the critical importance of book production to this community.

The map, split into four sections before being rejoined in a recent restoration, was discovered only in the summer of 1989 in an expedition to the North Dvina River region.

SEVERODVINA COLLECTION, NO. 807
Institute of Russian Literature, Academy of Sciences, Leningrad

RESPONSES FROM THE POMOR'E *[Pomorskie otvety]*, 1730s

Responses from the Pomor'e, written by the brothers Andrei and Semen Denisov in 1723 at the Vyg-Leksa Monastery, is a catechism of the fundamental dogmas of Old Belief. The form is a series of answers to 106 questions posed by the Archpriest Neofit, a representative of the official, synodal church. The book not only enunciates the fundamental differences between the old and new faiths. It is also the first Russian work to examine critically the reliability of historical sources (two books cited by church officials of the time are proven to be forgeries). Accepted as authoritative by Old Believers of all sects, the *Responses* was frequently copied over the course of two centuries. This manuscript is one of the earliest copies, as is evident in the relatively subdued style of ornamentation; later designs became far more elaborate. The page illustrated here represents the typical question-and-answer format of the book, with the response always beginning with an important initial letter.

The most recent owner of this book was the Old Believer elder from Pskov, M. A. Epifanov.

NOVGOROD-PSKOV COLLECTION, NO. 29
Institute of Russian Literature, Academy of Sciences, Leningrad

RESPONSES FROM THE POMOR'E *[Pomorskie otvety]*, late eighteenth century

Another, later version of the *Responses from the Pomor'e* illustrates one among the many theological issues discussed in the catechism, the *dvoeperstie,* or the Old Believer practice of using two, not three fingers to cross oneself. The marginal illustrations on the page shown depict various attitudes and usages of this blessing. Other areas of disagreement between the reformed and unreformed Orthodox were the singing of two, not three alleluias in the service, the shape of the cross (eight-cornered rather than four-cornered), and the spelling of Jesus's name. While these matters of ritual may seem too minor to have caused a schism, the Orthodox have always placed a special importance on the act of worship itself. Correct form was merely an outward sign of an inward intention, and worshipping God in the correct manner (in Russian, Orthodoxy is translated as *pravoslavie,* or "right praising") was considered essential to personal salvation.

LIFE OF ALEXANDER NEVSKY *[Zhitie Aleksandra Nevskogo]*, 1790s

The historical and hagiographical work from the end of the thirteenth century that treats the canonization of medieval secular leader Prince Alexander Nevsky (1220–1263) has survived in many copies and various redactions, including a reworking undertaken at the Vyg Monastery. This manuscript from the 1790s contains both the life and a liturgical service in honor of the saint, who was venerated for both his military and his spiritual exploits. The illumination, with its baroque ornamentation, elaborate ligatures, and color scheme of gold, green, and crimson, is characteristic of the Pomorian style of manuscript decoration. The text is a version of a redaction written in the sixteenth century by the Pskov scribe Vasilii-Varlaam.

The manuscript was acquired in 1972 from the heirs of Leningrad Old Believers.

INDIVIDUAL ACQUISITIONS, OP. 23, NO. 197
Institute of Russian Literature, Academy of Sciences, Leningrad

WORKS OF ANDREI DENISOV, 1810s

Andrei Denisov (1674–1730) was one of the founders and the first abbot of the Vyg-Leksa Monastery. Author of many sermons and homilies, he was the primary compiler of the *Responses from the Pomor'e*. He seems to have studied theology, rhetoric, logic, and poetics either in Kiev or in Moscow. His writings enjoyed unquestioned authority among the Old Believers of the priestless sect of Pomorians, and his works became models for all literature of the Vyg school of writing. Although Denisov's works were copied many times during the eighteenth and nineteenth centuries, few compendia have been preserved, and it is even rarer for a surviving copy to contain a likeness of the author. This manuscript was found in Pechora in 1972.

UST'-TSIL'MA NEW COLLECTION, NO. 302
Institute of Russian Literature, Academy of Sciences, Leningrad

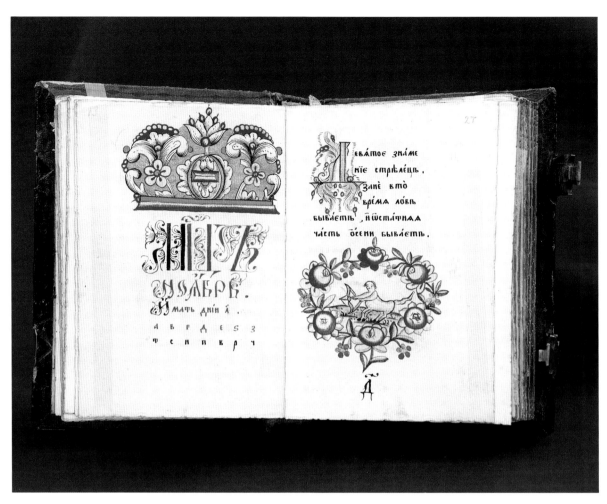

LITURGICAL CALENDAR *[Sviattsy]*, 1837

Sviattsy, a monthly calendar of church feasts, can appear separately, as this book does, or it can be included among the contents of other liturgical books. Days celebrating saints and church festivals are listed beginning with September 1, which, from the end of the fifteenth century until the reforms of Peter the Great, was considered the beginning of the new year. Special tables are included at the end for calculating the movable feasts of the Easter cycle. It is interesting to note that this book dates from 1837, the year the great poet Alexander Pushkin died following a duel. Pushkin, unlike the writers and artists of following generations, was raised in a world which was more familiar with French literature than with their own Old Russian traditions, and the "discovery" of this literature in the second half of the nineteenth century had an important influence on the course of Russian literature. This calendar, ornamented in the Pomorian style, opens each month with a depiction of the sign of the zodiac. Here the text for December reads: "The tenth sign is the Archer, for it is the season of game, as it is the end of autumn."

INDIVIDUAL ACQUISITIONS, OP. 25, NO. 124
Institute of Russian Literature, Academy of Sciences, Leningrad

BOOKS OF LITURGICAL MUSIC

In Russia church services are traditionally chanted, and liturgical texts are therefore usually accompanied by musical notation to aid the priest and choir in singing. The old East Slavic system of chant notation is called "hook-style" *(kriuki)*. The Old Believers still use this ancient system. In liturgical books, as in theological and polemical literature, the Pomorian style of ornamentation predominated among all groups of priestless Old Believers. Among the priested there was an equally influential style of ornamentation, developed in the textile town of Guslitsa, near Moscow. This style, characterized by a flamboyant palette with highly saturated colors, and an exuberant though not always very refined decorative sense, appeared in the last quarter of the eighteenth century and flourished until the 1920s. Examples of each style are shown here, as well as a highly individual and expressive work of popular art from the Caucasus.

The Old Believers so delighted in ornamentation that even those who used printed liturgical texts continued to commission hymnals to be hand-copied and decorated. The degree of adornment varies from the simple to the ostentatious, indicating that even people of small means would spend what money they had on these books. Ornamentation in hymnals shows a special affinity for birds, and the books here include both the mythological *sirin,* or bird with the head of a woman, and the humble barnyard rooster.

CHANT BOOK FOR SPECIAL LITURGIES *[Stikhirar'],* 1819

This collection of chants, one of the oldest types of musical books known, is dedicated to specific feasts and saints' days, and is arranged in calendrical order. The manuscript is decorated in the Pomorian style, with the proliferation of birds (including the mythological *sirin* bird in the center) and the characteristic color scheme of gold, green, and crimson indicating its origin at the Vyg-Leksa Monastery, the major center of manuscript production among the priestless Old Believers. The copying of manuscript books was done there principally by the inhabitants of the women's part of the community, on the Leksa River. It is difficult to say whether the existence at Leksa of a professional scribal workshop was a continuation of older traditions or not. While one occasionally runs across the word *pisitsa,* or female copyist, in Russian medieval writings, information about manuscript production in women's convents is scarce.

This chant book belonged to the Riga Old Believer I. N. Zavoloko, a connoisseur and collector of old manuscripts.

ZAVOLOKO COLLECTION, NO. 85
Institute of Russian Literature, Academy of Sciences, Leningrad

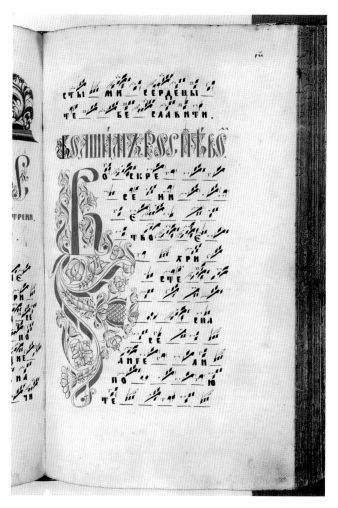

CHANT BOOK FOR THE LITURGY *[Obikhodnik]*, 1820s

The *Obikhodnik* is a liturgical book containing the chants for the priests' part of Vespers, Matins, and the Eucharist, as well as the tunes for hymns that vary by season. The lavishly ornamented illuminations, done in the Pomorian style, indicate the beginnings of the texts and accompanying hymns. It is characteristic of this style that initial letters are elaborate and outsized, often spilling over into the margins in a typically baroque manner.

MUSIC DIVISION
Library of Congress, Washington, D.C.

CHANT BOOK FOR THE LITURGY *[Oktoikh i obikhodnik]*, 1832–33

A manuscript consisting of two books bound together, the *Oktoikh i obikhodnik* exemplifies the multifaceted talent of its copier, Iosif Gariachev. He does not conceal his identity, and he names icon-painting as his profession. One of his acrostic poems appears at the beginning of the manuscript and his own musical setting of the text at the end. Gariachev even mentions the locale where he produced the manuscript, Kislye Mineral'nye Vody in the Caucasus. The depiction of a rooster instructing two children on how to sing Old Believer chant—the "ladder" is a scale—is unique and speaks of the folk artist's tendency to use images taken directly from his own life rather than from a stylistic tradition.

The manuscript probably remained in the Caucasus for over 150 years, until 1988, when it was given by the citizens of Piatigorsk to the Institute of Russian Literature.

BRAZHNIKOV COLLECTION, NO. 51
Institute of Russian Literature, Academy of Sciences, Leningrad

CHANT BOOK FOR THE LITURGY *[Irmologii],* Guslitsa, late nineteenth century

This songbook, which contains a common Orthodox hymn, is divided into eight voices, each voice into nine songs, and each song into three verses. This book comes from the priested sect of Old Believers, many of whom settled in the important textile center near Moscow called Guslitsa. It was an especially influential center of manuscript production, and this book shows a characteristic "Guslitsa style" of ornamentation. The songbooks of priested Old Believers differ from those of the priestless sects not only in the style of decoration, but also in the indication of pronunciation and vocalization of the verses. Therefore, choruses from the two sects never perform together for fundamental dogmatic, as well as stylistic, reasons.

OP. 3004
Church of the Intercession, Moscow

CHANT BOOK FOR HOLY DAYS *[Prazdniki]*, Guslitsa, 1888

This manuscript contains songs for the twelve most solemn holy days of the Orthodox Church calendar. The scribe, named Nazarii Shitikov, has ornamented this volume in the style of Guslitsa. Shitikov taught "hook-style" singing at the Rogozh Old Believer Community in Moscow, and in a note at the end of the book he relates that he learned the art of book production as a child, not far from Moscow. The note also indicates why he chose such an unusually large format and hand: "for a better reading [of the text] by a large group of singers." As a teacher of singing as well as choirmaster, he was only too well aware of the large choruses that gathered for holy days and of the problems that could follow if they were unable to read the music.

OP. 173
Church of the Intercession, Moscow

THE CULTURES CONVERGE

Government policy toward the Old Believers vacillated over the centuries. Catherine the Great and her grandson Alexander I tended to be lenient toward them. During their reigns, many of both priestless and priested Old Believers moved back into the cities of the empire, especially to Moscow, where certain trade privileges granted to them led to their emergence as the core of Russia's small mercantile class. The Preobrazhenie and Rogozh Old Believer communities in Moscow were centers of philanthropy, finance, commerce, and the production of old rite religious objects that served their coreligionists throughout the Russian Empire. But Nicholas I, alarmed by the sudden growth of the movement in the 1830s and 1840s, took decisive action against them. He shut down the Vyg-Leksa Monastery in Karelia and began enforcing laws that his predecessors had ignored. With the emancipation of the serfs in 1861, however, the government once again relaxed its persecution of the dissidents.

Despite official repression, the Old Believers grew steadily in number throughout the nineteenth century. Pavel Mel'nikov, the government official charged with the enforcement of statutes against the dissenters, estimated in 1860 that at least one-fourth of the Great Russian people were Old Believers. He was so impressed by their entrepreneurial spirit, high level of literacy, and strength of community life, that he predicted "the renovation of the Russian spirit will evolve only on the basis of the Old Believers' movement." Mel'nikov was not the only one drawn to this group: with the awakening interest in the peasantry that followed the emancipation, their culture became the object of study by historians, writers, and artists. Serge Zenkovsky, a noted scholar of the movement, remarked that "while the dogmatic details of their teachings were often rejected, even opposed, their messianic, national, and social approach to faith held great appeal for the peasantry and some urban groups of Russian society." These ideas were taken up by Slavophile writers in the 1840s and 1850s, and later on by Dostoevsky, who was especially persuaded of the idea of the messianic role the Russian people were to play in world history.

In addition, Old Believer merchants and laborers played an important role in the industrialization of the empire. They were predominant in the textile industry, and members of their merchant class were among the wealthiest in Russia. By the end of the nineteenth century, many of them had amassed considerable fortunes. Perhaps because they came from a tradition that revered books and icons, Old Believer merchants began to collect European as well as Russian art and books in the latter half of the century. Such notable collectors as Morozov, Shchukin, Riabushinskii, Tret'iakov, and Soldatenkov, whose collections may now be seen in the Hermitage, the Pushkin, and other Soviet museums, were all from Old Believer families.

Granted the right to practice their religion in peace after the 1905 Revolution, the Old Believer communities of St. Petersburg and Moscow experienced a cultural flowering. For the first time they were allowed their own schools, presses, and book shops. At last they were granted the same right to worship according to their conscience that the Muslims had gained long before. But it was a brief florescence. While as dissidents they had been courted by revolutionaries from Herzen to Lenin, the Old Believers proved to be conservative democrats, and after the October Revolution of 1917, many of the wealthier Old Believers fought in the White Army and later emigrated. Together with Old Believers who left Russia before the Revolution, they can be found in present-day settlements in Romania, Australia, Argentina, Alaska, Pennsylvania, and Oregon. The numbers of those who remained have dwindled in the seven decades of Soviet rule, though they are still strong in the Ukraine, in the North, and in Moscow. And the traditions that they did so much to protect and nurture for three hundred years have now passed into the mainstream of Russian culture.

MISCELLANY FOR THE COMMEMORATION OF THE DEAD *[Sinodik]*, 1840s

The *Sinodik* is a book containing names of the dead to be remembered at church services. Various types of such books are known to us. Since the seventeenth century, a common form would include a series of writings and homilies on the necessity of praying for the dead and on the efficacy of prayer by the living for sinners who had died. These writings often contain allegorical references to the seasons of the year and are illustrated with miniatures. The manuscript miscellany illustrated contains twenty-six illuminations and many initial letters done in a graphic style reminiscent of the ornamentation of printed books. It is likely that the nineteenth-century scribe studiously copied a seventeenth-century manuscript—and succeeded quite well. The copyist himself informs us of this in a postscript to the volume. The list of the dead to be remembered ends with the name of Tsar Mikhail Fedorovich, who died in 1645.

This manuscript was found in 1960 in a village near Lake Chud in southern Estonia.

PRICHUD'E COLLECTION, NO. 66
Institute of Russian Literature, Academy of Sciences, Leningrad

APOCALYPSE *[Apokalipsis tolkovyi]*, 1860–80

The Apocalypse, or Book of Revelation, was very popular among Old Believer peasants who, as they awaited the end of the world after the church schism of the mid-seventeenth century, argued about the reigning or soon-to-reign Antichrist. The text of the Apocalypse was often accompanied by lengthy commentary and imaginative illuminations, such as this one of angels pouring vials of God's wrath upon the earth. This manuscript was discovered in Karelia, and is notable for the distinctive quality of its gouaches, seventy-seven in all. The vividness of the palette and the abstract treatment of the picture plane is characteristic of peasant art, and is reminiscent of such avant-garde artists of the turn of the century as Goncharova and Kandinsky.

KARELIAN COLLECTION, NO. 248
Institute of Russian Literature, Academy of Sciences, Leningrad

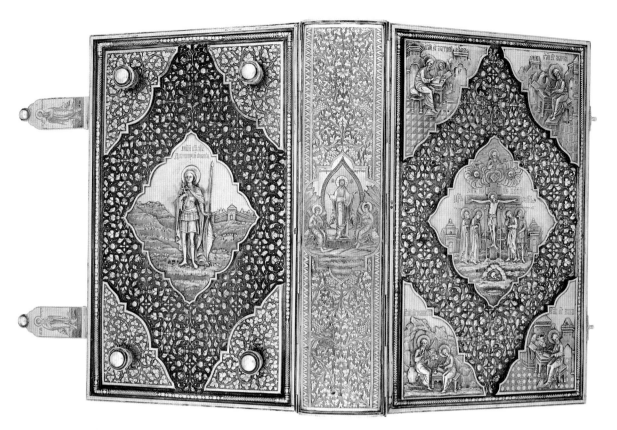

ALTAR GOSPELS WITH SILVER COVER *[Evangelie-tetr naprestol'noe],* Moscow, 1650

The Gospels were and are used in church services not only for the readings, but the book itself, as an object of worship, plays its role in the general service. It has its special place on the altar and, at the beginning of the service, it is held aloft for the congregation to behold. Such an edition of the Gospels is known as an Altar Gospels, and each church has one. They are usually elaborately covered in brocade and velvet, ornamented with precious stones and fresh water pearls, and at times even bound in covers made of gold or silver. This book, printed in 1650, was given its sumptuous cover as recently as the beginning of this century. The left or back cover is outfitted with four small feet to support the book, and on the right or front cover, the four Evangelists appear in each corner and Christ in the center. The richness of material and ornamentation is elegant witness to the flourishing of Old Believer culture, both spiritual and material, at that time.

OP. 472
Church of the Intercession, Moscow

THE PASSION OF CHRIST *[Strasti Khristovy]*, early twentieth century

Since the seventeenth century, apocryphal tales about the events of Holy Week have been widespread among Old Believers and among the reformed Orthodox as well. An example of the continuity of this tradition, this manuscript was copied at the beginning of the century by the peasant Vasilii Ivanovich Tret'iakov (1868–1930), who was from the North Dvina River region. Tret'iakov painted icons and works in the folk tradition, and examples of his paintings are found in a number of Soviet museums. He was not unique in the North Dvina region— around twenty such local painters and book illuminators are known from the late eighteenth through the early twentieth centuries. Here Tret'iakov depicts Christ washing the feet of his disciples. The man without a halo is identified by the artist as Judas.

This manuscript was discovered on an expedition to the North Dvina in 1975.

SEVERODVINA COLLECTION, NO. 353

Institute of Russian Literature, Academy of Sciences, Leningrad

CHANT BOOK FOR THE LITURGY *[Oktoikh]*, Moscow, 1913

At first glance, this book is easily mistaken for a manuscript, but in fact it is a printed version of a manuscript that was produced in 1834. Moreover, the book was printed on a government press, something unthinkable when the original was done by hand. But among the rights given to the Old Believers when the laws of religious tolerance were passed in 1906 was the right to print books and publish newspapers and magazines. While there are a large number of books printed by Old Believers before 1906, they were all produced illegally. This copy was given by the publishers to the Church of the Intercession at the Rogozh Old Believer Community, from whose original manuscript the book was produced.

OP. 56
Church of the Intercession, Moscow

CHANT BOOK FOR HOLY DAYS *[Prazdniki],* 1951

This kind of liturgical book contains hymns used on the chief feast days, of which there are twelve in the Orthodox Church, as well as hymns for other holy days or in remembrance of particular saints. In this chant book done in 1951, Christmas is depicted in a style that represents almost three centuries of manuscript-copying and icon-painting in the Latgalia region of the North. The hymnal includes sixteen paintings by the icon painter E. F. Ivanov, with a text executed by the well-known Old Believer elder D. D. Mikhailov, who also bound the book, using clasps of aluminum and furniture nails to decorate the exterior covers.

   This book comes from D. D. Mikhailov's descendants, who live in southern Latvia.

LATGALIAN COLLECTION, NO. 29
Institute of Russian Literature, Academy of Sciences, Leningrad

Checklist

1. Gospels *[Evangelie-tetr]*. Illuminated. 1490s. Folio (30 x 19.8 cm), 391 leaves. Nineteenth-century binding: boards covered in crimson velvet, with traces of two clasps. Miniatures and head-pieces in color and gold.

Institute of Russian Literature, Academy of Sciences

2. Acts and Epistles *[Apostol]*. Illuminated. Late fifteenth or early sixteenth century. Folio (28.5 x 19 cm), 170 leaves. Nineteenth-century binding: boards in embossed leather with two clasps. Contains sixteen miniatures. Headpieces and initials are done in color and gold.

Institute of Russian Literature, Academy of Sciences

3. Acts and Epistles *[Apostol]*. Moscow, 1564. Printed by Ivan Fedorov and Petr Timofeev Mstislavets. Quarto. Binding from the late eighteenth century: boards in stamped leather with two bronze clasps.

Library of Congress

4. Gospels *[Evangelie-aprakos]*. Illuminated. Last third of the sixteenth century. Large folio (37.8 x 26.4 cm), 441 leaves. Binding: boards in velvet with two clasps (the lower one is missing). Images of the Evangelists as well as initials and colophons done in color and gold.

Institute of Russian Literature, Academy of Sciences

5. The Life of Peter and Fevronia *[Zhitie Petra i Fevronii]*. Illuminated. Early seventeenth century. Quarto (17 x 13.5 cm), 22 leaves. Script. Cardboard binding in morocco leather with gold leaf stamp. Miniatures in color and gold.

Institute of Russian Literature, Academy of Sciences

6. Liturgical Calendar *[Sviattsy]*. Illuminated. 1636. Size is 8.7 x 3.5 cm, 208 leaves. Binding in boards is embossed leather with two clasps. Headpieces done in pen and filled in partially with gold. Restored in 1975.

Institute of Russian Literature, Academy of Sciences

7. Altar Gospels *[Evangelie-tetr naprestol'noe]*. L'vov, 1683 or 1690. Quarto. Contains the engravings of Evstafii Zavadov. Binding: boards covered with taffeta fabric, with superimposed gold figures of the Evangelists and Crucifixion scene, with two clasps. Several leaves at the end of the volume are damaged.

Church of the Intercession

8. Nomocanon *[Kormchaia kniga]*. Moscow, 1650–53. Quarto. Binding: boards in stamped leather with two clasps (the binding was restored in the nineteenth and twentieth centuries). Ownership inscriptions from 1787 and 1797 of the Moscow merchants M. D. Kirilov and V. A. Bol'shoi; in the nineteenth century the book belonged to Elisei Morozov.

Library of Congress

9. Autobiography of Monk Epifanii *[Zhizneopisanie inoka Epifaniia]* (second part). 1670s. Size is 10.3 x 8.3 cm, 46 leaves. No illustrations. Cardboard binding with cloth spine. The author's own writing, done while he was in prison.

Institute of Russian Literature, Academy of Sciences

10. Gospels of Tsarevna Sophia Alekseevna. Moscow, 1680s. Sophia Alekseevna was the sister of Peter the Great, and there is some evidence that

she helped to write this manuscript. Folio (31.5 x 20 cm), 486 leaves. Bound in boards in green velvet with superimposed bevels and centerpiece with figures of the Evangelists and the Crucifixion with mourners. Miniatures done in color and gold.

Institute of Russian Literature, Academy of Sciences

11. Law Code of 1649 *[Ulozhenie]*. Moscow, 1720s. Quarto, 380 leaves. Binding: boards in leather, restored in the 1980s. The text of the law code is written in the left-hand column of each page; in the right-hand column are entered the corresponding articles from regulations of the time of Peter the Great. A note at the beginning of the manuscript indicates that it was owned at one time by a groom of the Imperial Ministry of the Court Stables' Chancellory.

Library of Congress

12. Tale of the Solovki Fathers and Martyrs *[Povest' ob ottsakh i stradal'tsakh solovetskikh]*. Illuminated. Last quarter of the nineteenth century. Quarto (18.2 x 15.3 cm), 86 leaves. Binding: boards in stamped leather with two clasps. Contains forty-five miniatures and a framed color headpiece.

Institute of Russian Literature, Academy of Sciences

13. Works of Archpriest Avvakum. Illuminated. Late nineteenth or early twentieth century. Quarto (19.7 x 15.8 cm), 165 leaves. Binding: boards in stamped leather with traces of two clasps. Color miniatures; headpieces and colophon done in imitation of old manuscripts.

Institute of Russian Literature, Academy of Sciences

14. Map of Vyg-Leksa Monastery. Early nineteenth century. Size is 63.5 x 96.5 cm. Color panorama accompanied by explanatory legend of the area around the Old Believer monastery on the Vyg and Leksa Rivers. Discovered on an Academy of Sciences expedition into the countryside in the summer of 1989.

Institute of Russian Literature, Academy of Sciences

15. Responses from the Pomor'e *[Pomorskie otvety]*. Ornamented. 1730s. Octavo (17.7 x 11.4 cm), 456 leaves. Bound in boards with stamped leather, with remains of gold leaf and two clasps (the lower one is destroyed). The manuscript is illustrated with framed headpieces, other headpieces, colophons, and initials done at the Vyg Monastery; many illuminations throughout illustrating such things as signs of the cross.

Institute of Russian Literature, Academy of Sciences

16. Responses from the Pomor'e *[Pomorskie otvety]*. Illuminated. Late eighteenth century. Quarto, 408 leaves. Binding: boards in stamped leather with remnants of two clasps (on the back board there are traces of bronze hasps). Headings and initials done in the Pomorian style; in margins of some leaves are examples of two-fingered signs of the cross.

Library of Congress

17. Life of Alexander Nevsky *[Zhitie Aleksandra Nevskogo]*. Ornamented. 1790s. Quarto (19.3 x 14.8 cm), 62 leaves. Cardboard binding in blue velvet with gold clasps.

Institute of Russian Literature, Academy of Sciences

18. Works of Andrei Denisov. 1810s. Octavo (16.3 x 10.1 cm), 191 leaves. Bound in boards covered with leather. On leaf 11 (verso) in an ornamented headpiece there is an image of Andrei Denisov. Contains thirteen works by Denisov and his biography.

Institute of Russian Literature, Academy of Sciences

19. Liturgical Calendar *[Sviattsy]*. Ornamented. 1837. Size is 9.7 x 7.2 cm, 180 leaves. Bound in boards in stamped leather with remains of gold leaf and two clasps. Framed headpieces, other headpieces, initials, and colophon done in color and gold; signs of the zodiac.

Institute of Russian Literature, Academy of Sciences

20. Chant Book for Special Liturgies *[Stikhirar']*. 1819. Folio (32.7 x 20.8 cm), 456 leaves. Large Pomorian semiuncial. Binding: boards covered with crimson velvet, with traces of two clasps. Bordered headpieces, other headpieces, and initials in the Pomorian style, done in color and gold. Includes variants of the chants "In perevod," "In rozvod," "In rospev," and "Bol'shoi rospev."

Institute of Russian Literature, Academy of Sciences

21. Chant Book for the Liturgy *[Obikhodnik]*. Pomorian style ornamentation. 1820s. Quarto, 331 leaves. The binding was restored in the 1980s, using cardboard and glued marble paper, with leather spine and corners. Text contains references to the "Bol'shoe demestvo," "Demestvo pskovskoi prevod," "Put' Solovetskogo monastyria," "Kirilov perevod bol'shoi," and "Stolpovoe bol'shoe znamia." Contains the ownership stamp of Vikul Morozov.

Library of Congress

22. Chant Book for the Liturgy *[Oktoikh i obikhodnik]*. 1832–33. Quarto (21.8 x 17.2 cm), 216 leaves. Bound with boards in stamped leather with the remains of two clasps. Iosif Gariachev, writer and scribe. Several miniatures as well as ornamented headpieces, initials, and colophons done in color and gold.

Institute of Russian Literature, Academy of Sciences

23. Chant Book for the Liturgy *[Irmologii]*. Guslitsa style ornamentation. Late nineteenth century. Quarto, 260 leaves. Binding: boards in stamped leather with two bronze clasps. Headings and initials done in color and gold leaf.

Church of the Intercession

24. Chant Book for Holy Days *[Prazdniki]*. Guslitsa style ornamentation. 1888. Large quarto, 196 leaves. Binding: boards encased in stamped leather with two bronze clasps; four extensions on the back of the bottom board. The binding was restored in the third quarter of the twentieth century. Headings and initials done in gold leaf and color. At the end of the volume is a note about its acquisition for the Rogozh Old Believer Community and the payment to N. A. Shitikov, scribe of the manuscript, on September 2, 1891.

Church of the Intercession

25. Miscellany for the Commemoration of the Dead *[Sinodik]*. Illuminated. 1840s. Folio (37.3 x 20 cm), 72 leaves. Binding: boards in embossed leather with traces of two clasps. Twenty-six miniatures done in color; many headpieces and initials done in imitation of the style used in old printed books.

Institute of Russian Literature, Academy of Sciences

26. Apocalypse *[Apokalipsis tolkovyi]*. 1860s. Quarto (21.5 x 17.1 cm), 267 leaves. Bound in boards covered in leather with traces of two clasps. Contains seventy-seven color gouaches.

Institute of Russian Literature, Academy of Sciences

27. Altar Gospels with Silver Cover *[Evangelie-tetr naprestol'noe]*. Moscow, 1650. Quarto. Bound in an encasement of silver, ornamented with gold leaf, with images of the Evangelists and the Crucifixion (front cover), the Resurrection (on the spine), and Dimitrii Selunskii (back cover). On the two clasps are images of the Apostles Peter and Paul.

Church of the Intercession

28. Passion of Christ *[Strasti Khristovy]*. Early twentieth century. Quarto, 222 leaves. Bound in boards in leather with the remains of two clasps. This book copied, illustrated, and bound by V. I. Tret'iakov. Contains thirty-four miniatures in color and headpieces done primarily in pen and ink.

Institute of Russian Literature, Academy of Sciences

29. Chant Book for the Liturgy *[Oktoikh]*. Znamennoe penie Publishing House. Printing house of the Staff of the Moscow Military District, 1913. Quarto. Binding: boards in taffeta with gold stamping and two bronze clasps. This manuscript, with musical notation and ornamentation in the Guslitsa style, was written in 1834.

Church of the Intercession

30. Chant Book for Holy Days *[Prazdniki]*. Illuminated. 1951. Folio (24.6 x 17.8 cm), 477 leaves. Binding: boards in leather with two clasps from aluminum and nails. Sixteen miniatures done by the icon painter E. F. Ivanov. Text and binding done by D. D. Mikhailov.

Institute of Russian Literature, Academy of Sciences

Typeset in Galliard with Jaquish Ornaments by Brown Composition, Baltimore, Maryland, 1,000 copies of this catalog have been printed by Garamond/ Pridemark Press in Baltimore.

Designed by James Conner